Ancient Armour

Eli Taylor

Observations on the Use of the Sling, as a Warlike Weapon, Among the Ancients

Walter Hawkins

Coachwhip Publications
Greenville, Ohio

"Ancient Armour," by Eli Taylor
"Observations on the Use of the Sling," by Walter Hawkins
Copyright © 2013 Coachwhip Publications
No claims made on public domain material.
Front cover: Ancient Egyptian Battle
   of Kadesh depicted on frieze at Luxor
      © Amanda Lewis

ISBN 1-61646-197-7
ISBN-13 978-1-61646-197-3

CoachwhipBooks.com

ANCIENT ARMOUR
(PUBLISHED IN SIX PARTS)

ELI TAYLOR
(EDITOR, *THE FAMILY MAGAZINE*)

THE FAMILY MAGAZINE

1839

ARMOUR.

From the earliest period of history until the discovery of gunpowder, and the invention of firearms, frequent mention is made of *armour*, or means of personal protection from foes, either in single combat, or general battle. The extent, and manner of construction of this protection, has always varied in accordance with the advanced state of civilization, and the offensive weapons used, among nations where armour was worn.

The first Scriptural account of a complete *suit* of armour, (and this record is anterior to profane history,) is given in I. Samuel, xvii, 5—7, where the Sacred historian describes the armour of Goliah of Gath.

"And he had a helmet of brass upon his head, and he was armed with a coat of mail; and the weight of the coat was five thousand shekels of brass. And he had greaves of brass upon his legs, and a target of brass between his shoulders. And the staff of his spear was like a weaver's beam; and his spear's head weighed six hundred shekels of iron; and one bearing a shield went before him."

This description implies that the Philistines were, at that time, (1060 years before Christ,) full armed men; yet, the complete "man of mail," which the European knight of the twelfth century exhibited, was, doubtless, unknown among the ancients. But the armour of the European was but an improvement of the Asiatic, for, in the corroborative testimony of both sacred and profane writers, we have abundant evidence, that *body armour* originated among the people of the East. Even at the time of Goliah, armour was not uncommon, for, in the same narrative we find Saul in possession of a suit, which he offered to David when he received permission to go out and fight the giant Philistine.

We intend to give, in consecutive order, a series of literary and graphick illustrations of this subject, which, we doubt not, will prove highly interesting to the readers of the Magazine. Our sources for information are ample and correct. We commence with

HELMETS.

Of all kinds of armour, a strong defence for the head was unquestionably the most common, and perhaps the most early. The shield and helmet have indeed formed the only defensive armour of some nations.

When men began to feel the need of a defence for the head in war, they seemed in the first instance merely to have given a stronger make to the caps which they usually wore. Such caps were at first quilted or padded with wool; then they were formed of hard leather; and ultimately of metal; in which state they gradually acquired various additions and ornaments, such as embossed figures, ridges, crests of animal figures, horsehair, feathers,

a, b, c, Egyptian Helmets worn by Warriours; *d, e,* Caps of Egyptian Soldiers; *f, g,* Persian Helmets; *h, i, k,* Syrian; *l, m, n, o,* Phrygian; *p, q,* Dacian.

&c.; and also flaps to protect the neck and cheeks, and even visors to guard the face. Visors do not, however, appear to have been used by the ancient Orientals; nor do we know any helmet but that of the Phrygians with a ridge of crest. When the dress, or at least the war-dress, of ancient people consisted of skins, it was frequently the custom for the wearer to cover his head with the head-skin of the animal; and long after other dress was adopted for the body, it remained the custom among several nations to wear, as a war-cap or helmet, the skin of an animal's head, with the hair on, and in every other respect as like life as possible. The head-skins of lions, wolves, horses, and other animals, sufficiently grim in their appearance, and with hides of suitable strength, were preferred for this purpose; and the terrible effect of this defensive head-dress was increased by the teeth being exposed, so as to appear grinning savagely at the enemy. Now when such people began to find that more convenient war-caps might be invented, they were unwilling to forego the effect which their savage helmets produced, and therefore affixed the animal's head, and ultimately a representation of it, as conveniently as they could, to the top of their new war-cap. Count Caylus and Sir Samuel Meyrick concur in the opinion that this was the origin of crests and other annexations of helmets. Even the skins of large birds and fishes were employed in the same manner; and we have thus an easy explanation not only of the crest, but of the erect ears, horns, wings, &c., which we see in ancient helmets. The horsehair, which was anciently and is still displayed on helmets, admits of the same explanation. It arose from the custom of wearing the head of a horse with the mane remaining, either *proper*, or cut short so as to stand erect like a hog's bristles; the tail also being annexed. The Ethiopians and Libyans had horse-head helmets: their Egyptian neighbours gave up animal heads for helmets, but continued them as crests; the crest of the royal helmet among that people, being, according to Diodorus, the heads of the horse, lion, or dragon. Now Herodotus says, that the Greeks borrowed their helmets, as well as their shields, from the Egyptians. But those we have mentioned were far from being the only people who had animal-head helmets.

Of the Hebrew helmets, we only know that they were generally of brass; and that the helmet of the king was distinguished by its crown. It is, however, interesting to learn that metallick helmets were, so far as appears, exclusively in use among them. Homer's heroes have also, generally, helmets of brass. Whether the Hebrews had crests to their helmets or not, it is impossible to say distinctly. We do not think that the crest was a characteristick of oriental helmets; but as the royal helmet in Egypt had a crest—as the helmets of Asia Minor were sometimes crested—and as in the Trojan war a crested helmet was worn by the Trojans, and also, it would seem, by the Greeks—it is not unlikely that the crest was known to the Jews. Plumes we are not to expect; they were not used in the most ancient periods, and but sparingly in latter antiquity. Homer never mentions plumes; but often horsehair. So of Paris it is said:—

"He set his helmet on his graceful brows,
Whose crest of horsehair nodded to his step
In awful state."

In the combat which followed, Menelaus was dragging him along by his horsehair crest, when:—

"The broider'd band,
That under braced his helmet at the chin,
Strained to his smooth neck with a ceaseless force,
Choked him."

But, fortunately for him, this band, "though stubborn, by a slaughtered ox supplied," snapped, leaving the said helmet only in the victor's hand. It seems that in these crests the ridge was covered with hair from the mane of the horse, while other and longer hair hung dependent from the extremity behind; but the ridge often terminated in a horsetail when its surface had other ornaments. Meyrick seems to think that the horsehair was sometimes gilt, which is less unlikely than that, as he also supposes, this ornament was sometimes composed of wires of gold.

As we do not know the form of the Hebrew helmet, we shall add a few remarks concerning those of the nations who either were their neighbours, or with whom they were connected, or to whom they were subject at the different periods of their history; and whose helmets at such times they probably wore, or at least allowed the forms they exhibited to modify their own. They must certainly have been well acquainted with them.

EGYPTIANS.—In this country the kings and nobles only wore helmets of metal; the common soldiers wore caps of woollen or of linen strongly quilted.—There are specimens of these in our wood-cut. PHRYGIANS.—The Phrygian bonnet in peace, and the helmet in war, was the prevalent head-dress of the inhabitants of Asia Minor, and in Meyrick's opinion the helmet is one of the most ancient, and the same which was worn by the Trojan heroes in Homer. Its general form will be seen in our wood-cut; and the following particulars deserve attention, as they illustrate our preceding observations concerning the transmutation of a cap into a helmet. Its principal characteristicks were those of a cap with the point bent forward, and with long flaps descending to the shoulders. It sometimes appears as a mere cap of the most soft and pliable stuff, unable to support itself, and hanging down in large wrinkles; at others it appears to have formed a helmet of the most hard and inflexible substance—of leather, or even metal, standing quite stiff and smooth, and enriched with embossed ornaments. To many of these there are four flaps, which would appear to have been made from the leg-skins of the animals of whose skin the cap was originally formed; but in the lighter caps there are only a single pair of flaps, which are often tucked up and confined by a string around the crown. A flap of mail frequently descended from under the helmet to protect the neck and shoulders. The SYRIANS seem to have adopted, with some modification, the cylindrical helmet or cap of the Persians; but there is one, represented in our wood-cut, which is considered more peculiarly Syrian, and the resemblance of which, as Sir S. Meyrick remarks, to that of the modern Chinese is very great. They have alike a high, ornamental spike at the top: that which terminates the Syrian one is a lily, which, according to Herodotus, was the ornament which the Assyrians bore on the tops of their walking-sticks. The ASSYRIANS had helmets of brass.

The MEDES and PERSIANS.—As we are not stating minute distinctions, we may mention generally that the helmets, or "impenetrable caps," as Xenophon rather calls them, of the Medes and Persians, exhibit four principal forms in the accounts of ancient writers and in the sculptures of Persepolis: these are cylindrical, hemispherical, semi-oval, conical. To these also applies the remark concerning the origin of the form of the national helmet in that of the national cap. The cylindrical cap and helmet must, however, be particularly regarded as a national characteristick of the ancient Persians, the other forms being too general to be assigned as a national distinction. It is exhibited in the form of a cylinder of various height, with a somewhat wider diameter at top than at bottom, and resembling a hat without a brim—particularly such hats with broad crowns as were in use a few years since. It is either plain, or fluted, or otherwise ornamented; and we see it exhibited either simply, or in various combinations—sometimes as a diadem, often radiated at top, and variously embossed and ornamented, and encircling one of the round, semi-oval, or conical caps. This cylindrical cap or helmet became greatly diffused by the conquests of the Persians, and must have been well known to the Jews during the captivity, and while Palestine was a Persian province. Xenophon speaks of brazen helmets with white crests; but no crests appear in the sculptures of the country.—We need not particularly dwell on the helmets of the Greeks and Romans. These were, indeed, well known to the Jews in the later period of their history; but much that might be said concerning them has been anticipated in our first observations. The Roman helmet was borrowed from the Greeks with slight modifications. Of the more elaborate Greek helmet the cut of a Greek warriour, which will be given in our next number, will furnish a very fine specimen, which will be better understood by the eye than by technical description. It has three crests of horsehair from the mane, cut short and square, with a dependent tail. Some helmets had as many as five crests of this sort. The more common helmet of both the Greeks and Romans, being merely a scullcap without ridge or crest, but having at top a knob or button, and differing in no material respect from that of the mounted Dacian except that the latter has a spike instead of a knob.

THE FAMILY MAGAZINE.

ANCIENT ARMOUR.

Continued from our last number.

CUIRASES.

a, Egyptian; *b*, Phrygian; *c*, Dacian; *d*, Roman, Common Soldier; *e*, D. Officer; *f*, Do. Imperial.

In our last we gave a full description of *helmets*, or defences for the head of watriours, as used among various ancient nations. We now proceed to the subject of *body armour*, consisting of the cuiras, breastplate, corslet, girdle, skirt, greaves, &c.

When men had realized a means of protecting their heads by strong caps and helmets, they naturally began soon to think of extending the same protection to other parts of the body. It would be absurd to suppose that every nation adhered to the same rule of progression; but it may perhaps be stated as a general rule, with large variations, that the progressive kinds of armour were—

1. The skins of various animals, and even, in some countries, of birds and fishes.

2. Hides, mats, wood; linen or woollen padded or folded; strong twisted linen.

3 Leather bordered with metal.

4. Entire plates of metal; but as these were heavy and inflexible, various contrivances were resorted to in order to obtain the security which metal gives, without its rigidity, and without all its weight. For this purpose, the leather was covered with square pieces of metal, riveted on; or else, embossed pieces of metal were fastened on so as to protect the more important parts of the person, and to serve at once for ornament and use. Sometimes also, the defence was formed of bands or hoops of metal, sliding over each other, and therefore yielding to the motions of the body.

5. We then come to what is properly mailed armour, by which a higher degree of flexibility was obtained than a metallick covering might be supposed capable of affording. This armour was of several kinds. Leather, linen, or woollen, was covered with rings or with scales. The rings were of various kinds and sizes, and variously disposed. Sometimes they were fixed independently of each other, as in the very fine specimen of Phrygian mail which our wood-cut exhibits; in other instances, the rings were twisted into each other, like the links of a chain; and, in some cases, the rings were set edgewise, as shown in the Egyptian hauberks (fig. *a* of the above cut), which Denon copied from the walls of Carnac, and which, in Sir S. Meyrick's opinion, affords the earliest known specimen of this kind of armour. Scale armour was that which obtained the same effect by arranging small pieces of metal, cut into the shape of leaves, scales, &c., in such a manner that they fell over each other like the feathers of a bird, or the scales of a fish. This kind of armour had grown into extensive use long before it was adopted by the Romans, who regarded it as a characteristick of barbarians—that is, of any nations except themselves and the Greeks. In the time of the emperours, they were, however, led to adopt it from the Dacians and Sarma-

A Phrygian, in a coat of Ringed Mail.

A mounted Dacian in Scale Armour.

tians. This scaled armour was not, however, always of metal; for the last-named people had none such. They were without proper metals, and therefore they collected the hoofs of horses, and after purifying, cut them into slices, and polished the pieces so as to resemble the scales of a dragon, or a pine-cone when green. These scales they sewed together with the sinews of horses and oxen; and the body armour thus manufactured was, according to Pausanias, not inferiour to that of the Greeks either in elegance or strength. The Emperour Domitian had, after this model, a cuiras of boars' hoofs stitched together; and this, indeed, would seem better adapted to such armour than the hoofs of horses. With such armour as this of scales, or indeed that of rings, any part of the body might be covered; and, accordingly, we see figures covered with a dress of scale, ring, or chain armour, from head to foot, and even mounted on horses which have the whole body, to the very hoofs, clad in the same manner. Of this, our cut of a Dacian warriour on horseback is a curious specimen. The construction of such mailed armour had been brought to a state of astonishing perfection. In some instances, particularly in scale-armour, we see figures covered completely in suits fitted to the body with consummate accuracy, and displaying not only the shape of the wearer but even the muscular parts of the person; that is to say, the armour was so flexible that it yielded readily to the pressure of the muscles and to the various motions of the body.

Having thus noticed the various methods in which ancient armour was made, it is desirable to notice the parts of which it consisted.

The thorax or breastplate.—There is no question that this, as Sir S. Meyrick suggests, was the most ancient piece of armour for the protection of the upper portion of the body. When men began to extend to that the protection which the helmet had given to the head, a defence for the breast was naturally the first desired and attempted. This was the principal use of the *thorax*, which for a long time continued to be, under various modifications of form, the sole body-armour of ancient nations; and which, under further modifications, was used in addition to other pieces of armour, subsequently introduced. It probably originated with the Egyptians, among whom, according to Meyrick, it was the only body-armour; a position to which we apprehend that some exceptions must be allowed. It hung over the breast and shoulders, in the manner of a tippet; and was made of linen, several times folded and quilted in such a manner as to resist the point of a weapon. These linen pectorals came into extensive use among the neighbouring nations; and those of Egyptian manufacture were particularly valued. A linen thorax of this kind seems to have been worn in the Trojan war by the Lesser Ajax who—

"With a guard
Of linen texture light his breast secured."

Sir S. Meyrick thinks that the Persians were the first who gave a metallick character to the thorax; and it is also his opinion that it was the principal piece of body-armour among the Hebrews.

The Corslet, called by the Greeks *mithree,* was of various forms; and composed, progressively, of the sundry materials we have described. It was a sort of waistcoat, sometimes consisting of two compact pieces, one covering the front and the other the back, and commonly fastened to each other at the sides. At first these cuirases, whether compact or mailed, were cut short round at the loins; as in the cut of the Greek warriour, which illustrates many of the details we are now giving, for these short corslets continued to be worn by certain descriptions of warriours long after that more complete cuiras had been introduced, which followed the line of the abdomen; and which, whether of leather or metal, was, as we see in the Roman cuirases, hammered so as to fit exactly to the natural convexities and concavities of the body; with the natural marks of which, as of the naval, &c., it was often impressed. These cuirases were sometimes plain, but were often highly enriched with embossed figures, of common or precious metals, in wreathings, borders, animal heads, and other figures. The Romans, in particular, affected the Gorgon's head on the breast, as an amulet.

The girdle.—This was of more importance with the thorax only, or with the short corslet, than with the cuiras which covered the abdomen. Its use is seen in the cut of the Greek warriour; but it was often broader than it there appears. It was a part of their armour on which the ancient warriours set high value. It was often richly ornamented; and the gift of a warriour's girdle to another was a testimony of the highest consideration. Thus it is not forgotten to state that Jonathan gave his girdle to David; and we read in the Iliad, (vii. 305,) that when Hector and Ajax exchanged gifts, in testimony of friendship, after a hard combat together, the latter presented the former with his girdle. It is often mentioned in Scripture; and from its use in keeping the armour and clothes together, and in bearing the sword, as well as from its own defensive character, "to gird" and "to arm" are employed as synonymous terms.

The skirt or petticoat fell below the girdle, and with the short cuiras covered only the hips and top of the thighs, but with the long cuiras covered great part of the thighs. It was sometimes a simple skirt, but often formed a piece of armour, and frequently consisted of one or more rows of leathern straps, sometimes plated with metal and richly bordered or fringed. In many of the Roman cuirases, particularly those of superiour officers, the shoulders were protected in a similar manner.

The long corslet which covered the person from the throat to the abdomen, and, by means of the skirt, to the thighs, may be said to combine the several parts we have described, except the girdle, as may be seen particularly in figure f of the miscellaneous cut. They were in fact defensive tunicks; and having mentioned them above, we have only to repeat that they were, in different times and countries, composed of all materials we have specified at the onset. These several parts of armour when put on separately, or when united in such long cuirases as this, together with helmet and greaves, left only the arms, the lower part of the thighs, and the face, unprotected—and not always the face, as some of the ancient helmets had visors. But some parts being exposed, a step further was made by investing the body from throat to heel in a complete dress of mail, this step, however, was never taken by the classical nations of antiquity, it being in their view the attribute of such "barbarians" as the Sarmatians, Dacians, and Parthians.

Grecian Warriour.

Greaves were a kind of boots, without feet, for the defence of the legs, made either of bull's hide or of metal, generally brass or copper. The ancient greaves usually terminated at the ankle, and rose in front nearly to the top of the knee. It was open behind, but the opposite edges at the open part, nearly met when the greave was buckled, buttoned, or tied to the leg. There were some kinds that did not reach so high as the knee. This piece of armour was useful not only in combat, but for the purpose of guarding the leg against the impediments, such as iron spikes, &c., which the enemy strewed in the way, as well as to enable the warriour to make his way more easily among thorns and briers. It appears from ancient sculptures that greaves with the open part in front, and defending the calf rather than the shin, were sometimes in use. Sometimes a greave was worn on one leg only, and that was the left; that leg, and indeed the left side generally, being advanced in action on account of the buckler, which was borne on the left arm. Homer's heroes usually wore brass greaves; indeed the Greeks are continually called "brazen-greaved Achaians;" whence some suppose that this defence was first, and for a time exclusively, used by that people. The instance before us shows the contrary; and besides, greaves were worn by the Trojans as well as the Greeks. Thus, when Paris was arming for the combat with Menelaus—

"His legs he first in polished greaves enclosed,
With silver studs secured."

We learn from this, that in arming the greaves were first put on. The use of greaves was not confined to warriours, but they were worn by others, whose occupations required a defence against thorns. Thus, when Laertes is described as collecting thorns for a fence, it is said—

"Leathern were his greaves,
Thong-tied, and also patch'd—a frail defence
Against sharp thorns."

ANCIENT ARMOUR.

Continued from our last number.

In the two preceding numbers, we have given the reader, in detail, a minute description of the various kinds of *body-armour* used among the ancients, with their manner of construction, and mode of use, et cetera. We now proceed to the consideration of shields, spears, and other weapons of offence and defence, which properly come under the denomination of armour. Although the exact form of the various kinds of weapons used by nations of remote antiquity, cannot at the present day be corerctly determined upon, yet, viewing those now in use among the orientals, and using the evidence of ancient sculptures and paintings, we may fairly suppose that those descriptions given by learned antiquarians, and their accompanying pictorial representations, are undoubtedly very nearly correct.

In the next number we shall give a full description of the construction of shields and spears, accompanied with a cut of that splendid specimen of ancient art, the SHIELD OF ACHILLES, so beautifully described by Homer. The engraving is from a design by M. Quatremere de Quincy, whose authority in matters of this kind is of the highest character.

SHIELDS.

THE shield is unquestionably the most ancient and most general piece of defensive armour in the world. When it was first invented we cannot say; but it is mentioned in the Bible long before helmets or other defensive armour. It is the only defensive arm mentioned in the books of Moses. The Egyptians as usual claim the honour of the invention, and before it was discovered, men probably endeavoured to break the force of blows by doing what Diodorus tells us that the first kings of Egypt did—investing their persons with the skins of lions and bulls. Among the means for this purpose, the superior convenience and efficacy of such a contrivance as a shield, could not fail soon to occur to the mind; and accordingly, there is hardly any nation in which the shield, in some form or other, is not employed. Savages, who have not the least idea of such defences as the helmet or cuiras, are yet seldom found without the shield.

There are three if not four sorts of shields mentioned in Scripture; or at least, there are four names by which they are distinguished. The largest seems to be that called *tzinnah*, which was twice the size of the ordinary shield, as we learn from 1 Kings, 1. 16, 17; 2 Chron. ix. 16, where six hundred shekels of beaten gold were employed in the construction of the one, and three hundred shekels in the other. Formidable as this weight of metal for the *tzinnah* is, it probably does not give an approximating idea of its full weight, and still less of its size, as shields were almost never wholly of metal, but were of wood or skin covered with metal. We may suppose the *tzinnah* to answer to the larger kind of shields which were used in ancient nations. Concerning these and other ancient arms there are very complete indications in Homer's Iliad. Among his heroes, as well as in other times and nations, these larger shields were chiefly used by persons fighting on foot. Their length was nearly equal to that of a man, as we gather from several passages in that old poet; thus he says of Hector:—

> "So saying, the hero went, and as he strode,
> The bull-skin border of his bossy shield
> Smote on his heels and on his neck behind."

The same fact is implied in the intimations which we find of the bodies of the slain being carried on a shield; as in the famous injunction of the Spartan mother to her son, "Either bring back this buckler, or be brought back upon it." This refers also to the sentiment of honour connected with the preservation of the shield. It was natural enough for a man, when escaping, to desire to disencumber himself of such a burden and incumbrance as the larger kinds of shields were; and therefore the sentiment of honour was brought in, and made it disgraceful to lose the shield under *any* circumstances. The civilized Greeks and Romans, and the barbarous Germans, equally shared this sentiment. Among the latter, those who left their shields in the enemy's power, were excluded from civil and religious privileges, and often sought a release from ignominy in a voluntary death. The Hebrews participated in this feeling: and David, in his fine elegiac ode on the death of Saul and Jonathan, does not omit to mention this among the subjects of national regret, " Ye mountains of Gilboa, let there be no dew, neither let there be rain, upon you, nor fields of offerings : *for there the shield of the mighty is vilely cast away.*"

The length of these shields seems to show that they were either oblong or oval; and that they were hollow, which implies external convexity, we gather from their being described as "enclosing" or "encompassing" the body. Homer has such expressions, and so has David, which seems to prove the analogy in this respect. Tyrtæus, in one of his hymns still extant, is very precise on this point: "The warriour stands in the contest firm upon both feet : the hollow of the spacious shield covering, below, his sides and thighs, and his breast and his shoulders above." The manner in which these large heavy shields were used, may be collected by a comparison of the different passages in Homer. They were supported by a leathern thong which crossed the breast. So Agamemnon advises the warriours to "Brace well their shields," and foretels that before the approaching battle is over,

> "Every buckler's thong
> Shall sweat on the toil'd bosom."

And so in the battle itself, Pallas finds Diomede beside his chariot,

> "Cooling the wound inflicted by the shaft
> Of Pandarus; for it had long endured
> The chafe and sultry pressure of the belt,
> That bore his ample shield."

His wound was on the right shoulder; whence we may infer that the belt hung from that shoulder, and crossed the breast to the left side, where it was attached to the shield, which could, of course, be moved at pleasure, behind or in front. Lighter shields had sometimes a thong fastened to the handle, by which they were hung round the neck, and carried in any convenient position when not in use—upon the arm, at the back, or even on the hip. In action, and indeed often out of action, shields of different sizes were carried and swayed by means of a handle fixed to its inner surface; or, if large, by two loops or handles, through one of which the arm was passed while the hand grasped the other. In marching it must have been thrown behind, as we see from the instance of the margin of Hector's shield smiting his heels as he walked. In marching immediately to the assault, it was however sometimes turned entirely in front; the warrior then advanced, like Mars,

"Behind his broad shield pacing;"

but then the length of the shield obliged the owner to walk with short steps, like Deïphobus:—

"Tripping he came, with shortened steps, his feet, Shelt'ring behind his buckler."

This also shows its length, and seems at the same time to prove that its weight prevented it, under such circumstances, from being held at such a distance before the body, as to allow the free action of the feet. The weight of the larger kind of shield rendered it so great an incumbrance to a person otherwise heavily armed, that persons of consideration had an attendant, whose principal business it was to carry the shield of his superior. And this he did not merely when it was not wanted, but in action he sometimes marched before the warrior, to ward off the missiles which were aimed against him. The warrior of course sometimes took it himself when in close action. David was made Saul's armour-bearer. Jonathan's armour-bearer took a very active part in his master's exploit against the Philistine garrison. Goliath had an armour-bearer who carried his great shield before him. Arrian relates that Alexander had the shield which had been taken from the temple of the Trojan Pallas, carried before him in all his wars. The large shields were of great service when a body of men, acting in concert, joined their shields and opposed, as it were, a wall against the assault of the foe. In attacking fortified places the soldiers also joined their shields

The TESTUDO, or Tortoise-shaped Assemblage of Shields. From the column of Trajan.

over their heads, to protect themselves from the missiles which were discharged upon them by the besieged. This was called the *testudo*, or tortoise, because the soldiers were thus covered from the weapons of their enemies as a tortoise by its shell. This invention was exhibited in various forms, which ancient authors describe. That it was known to the Jews, appears from Ezekiel xxvi. 8, where the king of Babylon is described as lifting up the buckler against the city of Tyre. To render this junction of shields the more compact, the Roman legions had their *scutum*, with squared sides. It was of an oblong form (Polybius says, generally four feet long by two and a half broad) with a convexity given to its breadth. This shield, though it seems to have been reduced by the Romans, to a comparatively moderate size, may be taken as an average representative of the class of large shields, and therefore may be put in the same group with the Hebrew *tzinnah*. But the square form being intended to assist united action, we are not to expect to find it so prevalent among orientals and barbarians, who trusted less to the effect of combined action than did the Romans: and to an individual, a square shield with its sharp angles, is less convenient than one more or less of a rounded figure. Hence we seldom find shields other than round or oval, among the orientals, either ancient or modern; the Egyptians, however, had their shield of the shape of a tombstone, square at one end and round at the other.

From a sculpture at Thebes; contrasting the common Shield of the Egyptians with the round Shields of their adversaries.

Another Hebrew shield was the *magen*, which is the first that the Scripture mentions, (Gen. xv. 1,) and seems to have been that which was most commonly in use; being conveniently portable, and perhaps really more useful than the larger one; for although it did not protect the whole person, it could be turned with facility to ward off a coming blow or missile. This kind of shield is generally mentioned in connexion with arrows and swords; but the *tzinnah* with spears. It was about half the size of the latter, as we see that Solomon only appropriated three hundred shekels of gold for the manufacture of a *magen*, but six hundred for a *tzinnah*. Among the ancients the lesser shield seems to have been always used by horsemen and persons who fought in chariots, and occasionally by lightly armed footmen. The large shield was not the only one in use in the Homeric period. Neptune's advice to the Argives shows this :—

"The best and broadest bucklers of the host,
And brightest helmets put we on, and arm'd
With largest spears advance.————
———————— Ye then, who feel your hearts
Undaunted, but are armed with smaller shields,
Them give to those who fear, and in exchange
Their stronger shields and broader take yourselves."

And again :—

"With many a stroke
The bull-hide shields and lighter targets rang."

Perhaps, however, there was not such a contrast of size between the smaller and larger shields mentioned here, as between the *tzinnah* and *magen*. The latter is the shield which the present text mentions, and is thought by Gesenius to be analagous to the Roman *clypeus*. In this opinion we concur, because both seem to have been shields of average form and size. The Roman *clypeus* was a medium-sized shield, round, oval, or hexangular in figure; and had sometimes, a boss in the centre, as had the Hebrew *magen*, to which bosses are assigned in Job xv. 26—"The thick bosses of his bucklers." The central boss, which was a kind of projecting dagger, does not, however, seem to have been peculiar to any one kind of shield. It rendered the shield at the same time an offensive as well as a defensive weapon, and was of great use in bearing down the enemy in close fight. The shield of Agamemnon had twenty-one bosses—twenty surrounding bosses, and one in the centre.

The Hebrews must have had a considerable variety of shields; for besides these two, which occur most frequently, there are others of which we know nothing distinctly; but may infer that the different terms describe peculiarities of form and size. One of these is the *sohairah*, which, from the etymology, would seem to have been of a round form, which was and is a very common shape for the smaller kind of shields, and sometimes for the larger, as will appear by our cuts. It may well be taken as the

Roman Combat with the Spear and the small round Shield (called *parma*.) From a Bass-relief at Pompeii.

type of the Roman shield called *parma*, a small round shield much used by the cavalry and light-armed foot, and now very common in the east. Another is the *shelet*, (which occurs only in the plural,) and as it appears, from a comparison of parallel passages, to be sometimes used as synonymous with *magen*, we may infer that the former was essentially the same as the latter, with some small variation of make or ornament. See, for instance, Sol. Song, iv. 4—" Thy neck is like the tower of David, builded for an armoury, whereon there hang a thousand bucklers (*magen*,) all shields (*shiltai*, sing., *shelet*) of mighty men." The last clause is evidently a repetition of the preceding, *shelet* being used as a verbal change for *magen*. We do not notice the *kidon*, translated "target" and "shield," in 1 Sam. xvii. 6, 45; because it is more than doubtful that anything of the kind is intended.

ANCIENT ARMOUR.

SHIELDS.
(Continued from our last number.)

Having noticed in detail the various kinds of shields used by the ancient oriental nations, we now proceed to a brief description of their construction, and the materials of which they were formed.

A great portion of the shields described in Homeric verse, as well as noticed by subsequent ancient writers, were formed of wood and steel,

Form and manner of using the Roman Shield, as contrasted with those of the Barbarians. From the column of Trajan.

such material is used among some barbarous nations, when weapons of defence of this character are brought into requisition. Xenophon mentions Egyptian soldiers in the Persian army bearing "long wooden shields which reached down to the feet;" and according to Plutarch in his life of Cammillus, the wooden shield was in use among the Romans at the time of that general. They were made of two planks glued together, covered with linen, and then with raw hide. Around the whole circumference was fastened a rim of iron or brass, invulnerable to the strokes of the sword. Sometimes a shell of metal overlaid the other materials, thus rendering the shield doubly strong. But the material most in use, was the hides of bulls, doubled or tripled. According to Homer, the shield of Hector was of this kind, as well as those of most of that poet's heroes, both Greeks and Trojans. They were often anointed with oil, to prevent them from injury either of heat or wet, and it was to this practice that Isaiah alluded, when he said, "Arise ye princes, and anoint the shield;" thus practically admonishing them to keep their armor in readiness and order.

These bull's-hide shields were often rimmed with metal, as represented in the foregoing pictured combat. And they were also, like the wooden shields, sometimes *plated* with metal. Homer, with his usual perspicuity of detail, thus describes the shield of Ajax, when he battled with Hector:

"Ajax approached him, bearing, like a tower,
His sevenfold brazen shield, by Tychius wrought
With art elaborate; like him was none
In shieldwork, and whose home in Hyla stood;
He framed the various shields with *seven hides*
Of fatted beeves all plated o'er with brass."

* * * * *

Hector's spear—

———"Struck the shield of Ajax; through the brass
Its eighth integument, through six of hide
It flew, and spent its fury on the seventh."

Thus foiled by the great strength of the shield, Hector afterward—

———"Retiring, heaved
A black, rough, huge stone-fragment from the plain,
Which hurling at the sevenfold shield, he smote
Its central-boss; loud rang the brazen rim."

We often read in sacred history of brazen shields, and "shields of gold," (belonging to Solomon,) but it is probable that most of them were merely plated with the various metals These plates were kept polished, and when not in use, the shield was secured in a leathern case, to prevent rust and tarnish. Yet solid metal shields were sometimes used. Alexander the Great, had a body of soldiers who bore silver shields, and it is said that Alexander Severus had some men with golden shields. That the latter were solid, is extremely doubtful. The ancients were very fond of ornamenting their shields with various devices, such as beasts, birds, men, flowers, &c.; and even had historical subjects and scenes of social life embossed or engraved upon them. Of the latter kind of embellishment, were the ornaments upon the famous shield of Achilles, a description of which we intended to introduce here, but have deferred it till a future number.

Of other individual shields mentioned by Homer, none next to that of Achilles, was more remarkable than that of Agamemnon.

"His massy shield, o'ershadowing him whole,
High wrought and beautiful, he next assumed:
Ten brazen circles bright around its field
Extensive, circle within circle, ran;
The central boss was black, but hemmed about
With twice ten bosses of resplendent tin.
There, dreadful ornament! the visage dark
Of Gorgon scowled, bordered by Flight and Fear,
The loop was silver, and a serpent form
Cerulean over all its surface twined—
Three heads erecting on one neck, the heads,
Together wreathed into a stately crown."

The following cut represents ancient Persian shields and spears, from sculptures at Persepolis. For what purpose the appendage from the belt of the third figure was used, is doubtful, for it seems an uncouth form for a shield.

Ancient Persian Shields and Spears.

Although the Greeks, ever jealous of honor and glory, claim to be the *inventors* of armor of every description, as well as every other production of genius, yet it is highly probable from the testimony of sacred writ and concurring profane history, that the Hebrews were skilful in many arts of this nature, when the Greeks, a weak colony, first landed upon the shores of Europe. Other eastern nations were also well acquainted with the use and construction of armor, as is evident from the sculptures now extant, that were executed when Greece was in her infancy. The subjoined engraving represents an ancient Persian horseman, bearing a spear and shield, himself and horse protected by coats of mail.

Persian Horseman with Spear and Shield.

SPEARS.

These weapons were used in the offensive as extensively as the shields were in the defensive, and no warrior was completely accoutred for battle without his spear or javelin. Among the most savage nations, they were formed simply of a stick of wood sharpened and hardened in the fire; but among nations more advanced, improvements were made, and a stone or metal point was added, which rendered it more durable and destructive. Among the savages of our own country, the arrows are tipped with a kind of flint-stone. Sometimes the spear was pointed with horn, fish-bones, &c., where the use of metal was unknown. Among the ancient Greeks, brass and copper were used prior to the adoption of iron; and Homer frequently makes mention of the "brazen spears" of his heroes. In one instance he says of the spear,

"Rough-grained, acuminated sharp with brass."

Herodotus says that the Massageta had their arrows and spears pointed, and their battle-axes edged with brass. He also remarks that some were made entirely of brass, and we may infer that such was the case with some of the nations with which the Hebrew writers were acquainted, or perhaps with the Hebrews themselves, as frequent mention is made in scripture of the "glittering spear." The "target" (lance) of Goliath is described as "brazen," and yet it is evident from other passages, that iron and steel were afterward used.

Of the spears used by the Hebrews, but little is known, but they probably varied very little in their construction from those of surrounding nations. Like other warriors, they had two kinds, one intended to be hurled at the enemy when at a distance, and the other for giving thrusts during a close personal attack. In each case the shield was successfully used in the defensive, unless the spear or javelin was thrown with such force as to cleave the shield, and thus wound its bearer. The same kind of spear was often used for both purposes, and when two horsemen approached each other for combat, they commenced the attack by throwing their spears at each other. Their next aim was to recover their weapons thus thrown, and then commenced a close combat. Whoever first recovered his spear had a decided advantage over his antagonist, and hence *agility* was one part of an ancient warrior's military education. Homer often mentions the fact that his heroes retained, during continuous battles, the same favorite spear, and as it would generally be easier for one to recover the spear of the other, sooner than his own, if ineffectually thrown, it can be accounted for in no other way, than that it was a general understanding among combatants that each should use only his own.

Some warriors, remarkable for their prowess and strength, sometimes went into battle with two spears. Such was the case with Goliath. He carried one spear behind his buckler, and the other in his right hand. One was undoubtedly a lance, intended to be thrown at the enemy; the other handle, which is represented as being of the size of "a weaver's beam," was intended for close contest. The former may have been intended as a reserve, in case one was lost. The javelin and spear both varied in length as well as weight, and there was no definite size for either. Homer says of Hector,

> "Eleven cubits length
> Of massy spear he bore, its brazen point
> Star-bright, and collared with a ring of a gold."

Different ancient authors describe the spear of many of the ancient Macedonians as being of an immense length, some sixteen cubits, or eight yards. Joshua's spear must have been of great length, for it served as a signal at the time of the ambuscade in the affair of Ai.

As many of the *costumes* as well as *customs* of the ancient Asiatics are still preserved among the people of the east, we subjoin a group of modern oriental shields and spears, which undoubtedly give a very fair representation of those used among the ancients.

We shall conclude our notice of spears and shields at the commencement of our next number on ancient armor, and proceed to a description of other weapons, and various standards in use.

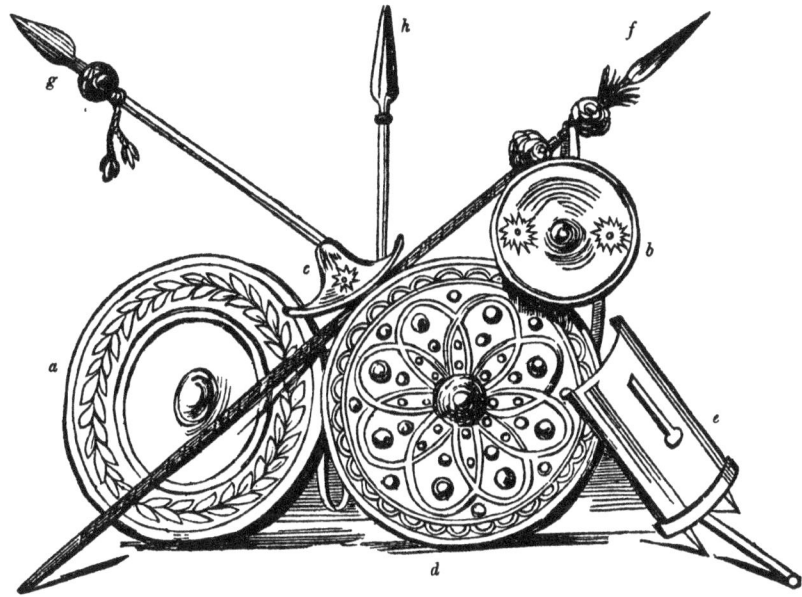

a, large Arabic shield; *b*, small do.; *c*, side view of the same; *d*, large Turkish shield; *e*, Mameluke shield; *f*, Arabian spear; *g* Turkish; *h*, Mameluke.

ANCIENT ARMOR.

Ancient Persian combat, showing how the Spears were used. From bas-reliefs at Nakshi—Roustan.

SWORDS.
(Continued from last number.)

In our last, we noticed the manner of using the long and short spear, for close combat, or for hurling. Among the Romans, a small kind of spear, or dart, was frequently used, not more than three feet in length, and an inch thick, with a point about four inches long. The point was tapered so fine, that it bent at the first stroke, and hence the enemy could not use it in return. They were carried by the light-armed horsemen of Rome, each having a number of them in the left-hand, to be thrown as occasion might require. Such darts were undoubtedly known among the Hebrews, and were, probably, the kind used by Joab, who, it is related, had *three* in his hand, and pierced the heart of Absalom with them as he hung in the tree. As we have before remarked, it required much skill to use the spear, javelin or dart successfully, and the scene of a combat with these weapons must have been peculiarly striking. Virgil says of one of his heroes:—

"Poised in his lifted arm, his lance he threw:
The winged weapon, whistling in the wind,
Come driving on, nor missed the mark designed."
* * * * *
"Thick storms of steel from either army fly,
And clouds of clashing darts obscure the sky."

We will conclude our notice of carried armor by a brief description of the *swords* used by the ancients, and also some now in use among the orientals.

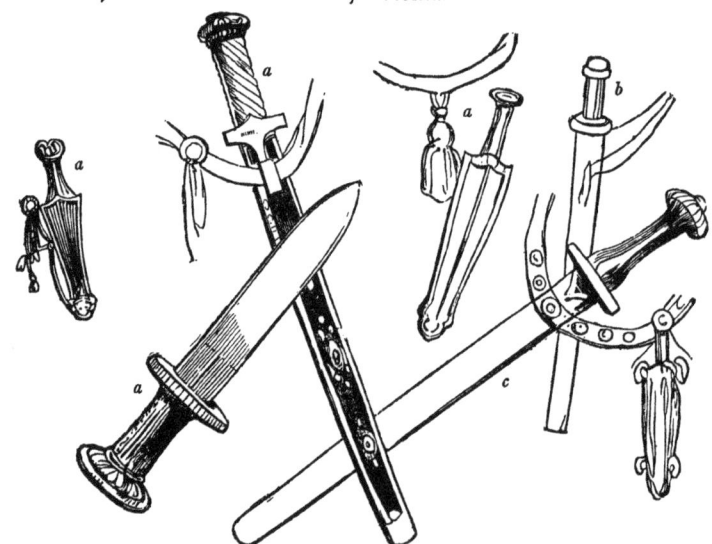

Ancient Persian Swords and Daggers.—From sculptures at (*a*) Persepolis, (*b*) Shiraz, (*c*) Takht-i-Bostan.

Although swords are named among the first warlike weapons in the scripture, it is by no means probable that they were of such early invention as the spear and shield, the bow and the dart, for of no other material than metal would they be efficient in warfare. The working of metals implies civilization or demi-civilization, and hence it is that among savage nations, the sword, even at the present day, is unknown. We read that Simeon and Levi did much execution at Sechem with the sword, and that Jacob defeated the Amorites with the sword and bow. These are the earliest records of the use of this instrument, but as anciently as the siege of Troy, they were in common use, according to Homer, and constituted an essential part of a warrior's armor. They were generally of brass or copper, and indeed the reader of the Iliad will observe, that almost every kind of metal weapon or instrument, were constructed of the former metal. It is probable that iron was not then in general use, and hence the universal employment of brass. The great sword of Achilles was made of this material, and they were not unfrequently splendidly decorated. Of Agememnon it is said:—

"He slung his sword
Athwart his shoulders; dazzling bright it shone
With gold embossed, and silver was the sheath
Suspended graceful in a belt of gold."

Ancient Swords and Daggers.—From Montfaucon. *a*, Greek; *b*, Roman; *c*, Ancient, but uncertain; *d*, Dacian.

Long subsequent to the time of Homer, the swords of the Greeks and Romans continued to be of copper. Specimens of this metal, supposed to have belonged to the Phenecians, and subsequently the Carthagenians, have been dug up in various countries; and in England and Ireland, specimens have been found, similar to those discovered at Cannæ, where it is known that the Carthagenians sustained a great overthrow and terrible slaughter.

In the British museum are specimens found in Palestine, and supposed to have belonged to the Israelites after their possession of Canaan, which very much resemble the Roman swords in the centre of the group in the preceding engraving, with the exception of the cross-bar or guard. These weapons vary in size, some being merely a dagger twenty inches in length, and others, from three to four feet long. Of the latter size, many were found in Ireland. The copper swords which have been discovered, are generally alloyed with some other metal, which makes them quite hard, and susceptible of a fine polish. Indeed, it is the opinion of some, that these swords were superior to iron, until the tempering of steel was employed.

As a general rule, the swords of ancient civilized nations were straight, and those of barbarians curved. The cavalry used long swords, but not such thin, keen weapons as are known to moderns. As the forms of ancient weapons are still retained among the people of the east to a great extent, we subjoin a group of such swords and daggers as are in use among them.

The Egyptians generally used cutting-swords, although straight ones and daggers have been found among them. The ancient Israelites, also, had straight swords and daggers; the former

Modern Oriental Swords and Daggers. *a*, Syrian Sabre; *b*, Syrian Dervish Sabre; *c*, Turkish Sabre; *d*, Dagger of the Prince Royal of Persia; *e*, Albanian Knife Dagger; *f*, Yataghan of a domestic of the Turkish Grand Vizier; *g*, Janissary's Dagger; *h*, Bedouin Arab's Dagger and Sheath.

were often two-edged, and were girded upon the thigh. The ancient Persians wore their swords suspended from a belt on the right side, and Heroditus mentions golden swords as having been captured from the Persians. These were probably only inlaid with gold. The early Greeks wore their sword under the arm-pit, so that the pummel touched the nipple of the breast; it hung by a belt, and its length was that of the arm. Some were for thrusting, others for cutting; and the latter sometimes had the edge on the inner curve. Their hilts were of ivory and of gold, with occasionally a hand-guard or cross-bar. The Romans wore the sword on the right thigh, that it might not obstruct the free use of the buckler, yet this rule was sometimes departed from. The Bedouin Arabs, more than any other of the eastern nations or tribes, retain the customs of the patriarchal times, and it is supposed that the dagger (*h*) given in the preceding cut is the most ancient of any, and was probably known in the time of Joseph. We will now proceed to notice other implements of war, used by the ancients.

Balista prepared for the discharge of a stone.

Catapulta prepared for the discharge of an arrow. From Montfaucon.

In II Chronicles, chap. xxvi. verse 15, we find it recorded, that Uzziah "made in Jerusalem engines, invented by cunning men, to be on the towns and upon the bulwarks, to shoot arrows and great stones withal." This undoubtedly refers to the *balistæ* and *catapultæ* of the Greeks and Romans, and as they are not mentioned by Homer, nor any of the writers prior to the time of Uzziah, (eight hundred years before Christ) we must, notwithstanding the general obtuseness of the Jews in such matters, believe that these "engines" were the "inventions" of, and not adopted by, Uzziah's "cunning men." Diodorus says, that had the besiegers of Nineveh, in the time of Sardanapalus, possessed these engines, with battering rams, that siege would much sooner have been brought to a close.

Of the construction of these machines, (some of which are still extant,) Pliny and others have given descriptions. The leading principles upon which they operated were those of the cross-bow, the recoil of twisted ropes, and the sling. The above cuts illustrate those acting upon the first two principles. The acting power lies in two coils of twisted rope, set apart from each other, into which are inserted, horizontally, the ends of two strong levers, the remoter ends of which are connected by a strong rope or ligature. Thus a gigantic cross-bow is formed, which, when the two arms or levers are drawn toward each other, increase the tension of the twisted ropes, and give a tremendous recoiling power, applicable alike to a stone or dart.

Head of the Catapulta, showing the rope, levers, and springs of twisted rope, by which the discharge was effected.

There was another machine, called *Onager*, or sling, which power was also given by ropes. Two perpendicular beams, set apart, were connected at top, by two strong cables, between which was inserted a large, crooked, tapering beam. When the small end of this beam was drawn toward the ground, it had an almost overpowering tendency to recoil upward. When a pear-shaped bag of stones had been hung at this end, the beam was released, bounded up, and discharged its burden with immense force at the enemy.

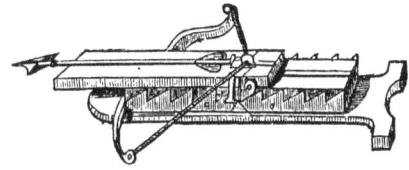

Scorpion.

The Scorpion was a smaller instrument, for the discharge of arrows, and was essentially a cross-bow, without the power of coiled ropes, as may be seen by the above engraving. The same machine was used by the ancients for throwing pebbles and larger stones.

These engines were used in great numbers, in besieging cities, and in the defence of the same. The Romans took upward of two hundred of them, large and small, from the Carthagenians; and at the siege of Jerusalem, the besieged had nearly four hundred of these machines, great and small, which they had taken from the Romans. Those used by the latter at that time, and particularly those of the tenth legion, were much stronger and more efficient than those of the Jews, some of which would throw huge stones to the distance of a quarter of a mile, and sweep a whole file of men, from one end to the other. Josephus who was present at the siege of Jerusalem, states, that a man standing near him, had his head knocked off by one of these stones, projected nearly three furlongs.

Battering Ram. From the Arch of Severus.

Another engine of war, peculiar to the Romans, was the Battering-ram, used for demolishing fortresses, and making breaches in the walls of cities, to let besiegers in. The place of its invention is not positively known, although it is highly probable that the Babylonians have the honor. It is mentioned in sacred history, only in Ezekiel, where it is said Nebuchadnezzar used

used them against Jerusalem. From Babylon the Tyrians learned its use, when the same monarch besieged that city, and from them it is probable the Romans obtained their knowledge of it.

The name is derived from the manner of its use, representing the butting of a ram. There were three kinds of battering rams; one, acting upon rollers, as represented in the foregoing cut; another suspended, like a scalebeam, by cables or chains, in a frame of strong timber; and another used by manual exertion alone, without suspension or other contrivance.

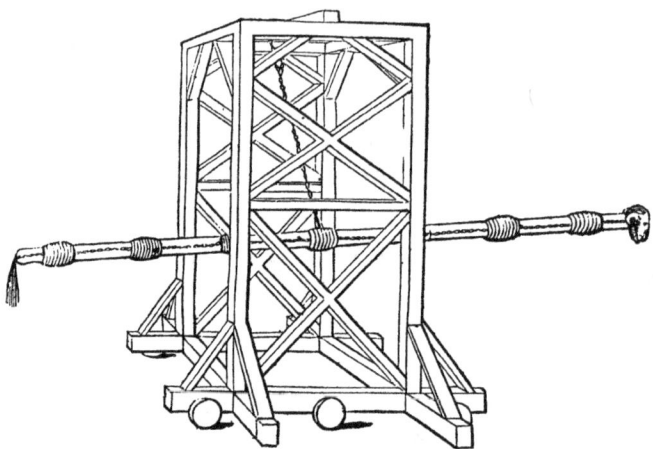

Suspended Battering Ram.   From Grose's Military Antiquities.

The first was worked with more precision and force, but with greater labor; the second was was worked very easily and powerfully, and the third was used only for demolishing weak objects. Josephus says, that at the siege of Jerusalem many of the Roman rams were destroyed by fire being thrown upon them from above; others were rendered almost powerless by sacks of wool being let down to oppose their blows, and large masses of rocks were thrown upon them, in many instances breaking off the heads.

We shall conclude the whole subject in the next number, by a literary and graphic illustration of various kinds of standards used among the ancients, including those of the twelve tribes of Israel.

ANCIENT ARMOR.
(Concluded.)

STANDARDS.

Although standards may not properly be classed under the head of armor, yet among civilized and demi-civilized nations they form a portion of the munitions of war, and hence we introduce a brief notice fo them, in concluding our article upon the armor of the ancients.

History furnishes many instances of the origin and use of standards among the various ancient nations, but the invention of them is generally accredited to the Egyptians. It is an undoubted fact, that of all nations, the Egyptians earliest exhibited a strong organized military force, and hence the reasonable conclusion that they were the first that made use of ensigns or standards. Diodorus, one of the earlier historians, informs us, that the most prevalent standard among the Egyptians was the figure of some animal at the head of a spear. Egyptian sculptures and paintings, in the tombs of their kings, exhibit other kinds of standards, the most common of which we give in the subjoined engraving.

Egyptian Standards.

The early Greeks had a piece of armor at the end of a spear for their standard. Agamemnon, according to Homer, used a purple veil. The Athenians subsequently adopted the olive, the owl, and the figure of their tutelar deities. The Persians had various kinds of ensigns, but the most common was a golden eagle. Quintius Curtius mentions one, as representing the sun, enclosed in a crystal globe, and made a splendid appearance above the royal tent. Among the sculptures at Persepolis, which are of ancient origin, standards are seen of various kinds: one kind consisted of a short staff, terminated at top by a ring, divided in twain, and having a cross-bar, to which enormous tassels were suspended. Another kind consisted of five globes upon a cross-bar, and were undoubtedly intended to represent some of the heavenly bodies which were anciently objects of worship in Persia.

The use of standards was and is, to form a focal or rallying point for the soldiers, and in most cases their courage remains strong so long as they can see their standard erect, or their flag fluttering in the breeze.

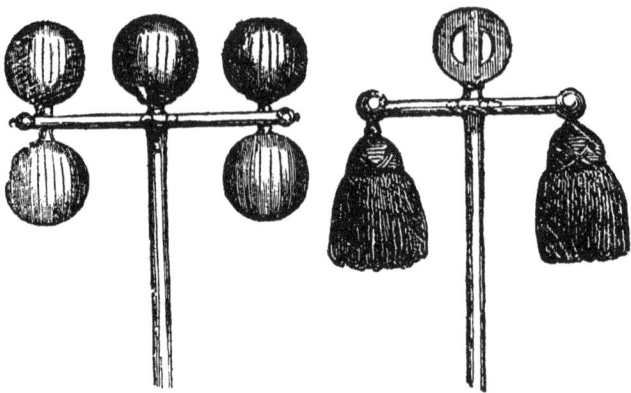

Persian Standards.

Such being the case, it matters not what may be the form or material of the ensign, and it is said, that for several centuries prior to the Mahometan conquest of Persia, that the proper royal standard of that country was a blacksmith's leathern apron, around which they at one time gathered, in opposition to the tyranny of Zohauk. Such has been the origin of many national standards, when the first thing that presented itself was reared for a rallying point. It is related that the most ancient standard of the Romans, was a bundle of hay; and thus originated the horse-tail standards, surmounted by a crescent, as used by the Turks of the present day.

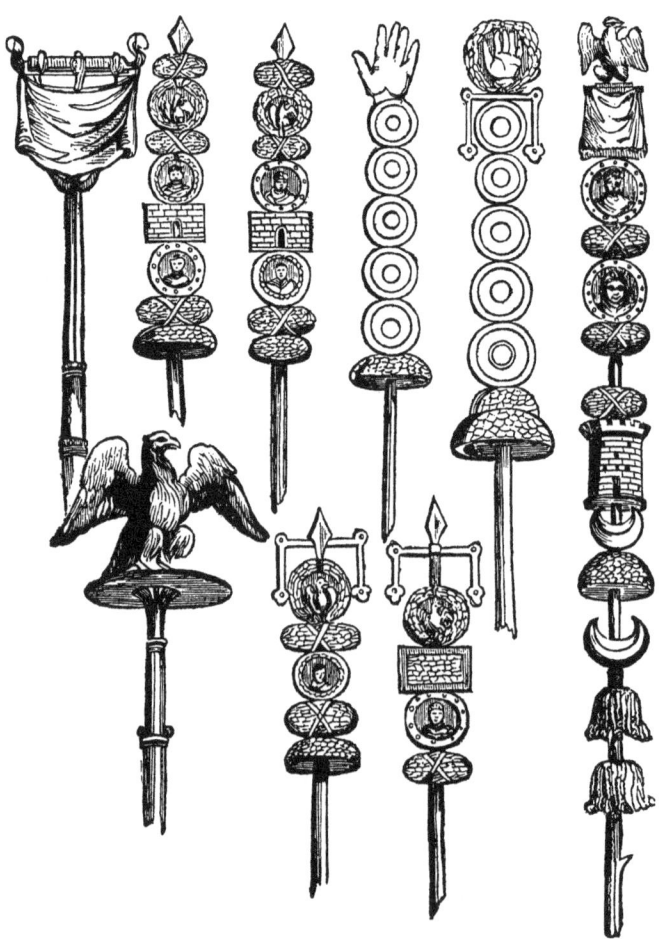

Roman Standards.

The ancient Romans had quite a variety of standards. As we have already mentioned, the first was merely a bundle of hay; afterward they adopted a spear, with a cross-piece at top and surmounted by the figure of a human hand, and below, a small oval shield, made of gold or silver. On this shield deities were engraven, and after the subversion of the republic, effigies of the emperor were inscribed thereon, and were held in great veneration. According to Dr. Meryck, each division of the Roman army had its peculiar standard. That of a legionry was a silver eagle with expanded wings, surmounting a spear, and grasping a thunder-bolt. The place for this standard was in the centre, near the the general. The flag of cavalry was a square piece of cloth fixed upon a cross-bar at the end of a spear. An infantry flag was red, a cavalry one blue, and that of a consul white.

Among the Persians the standard was often borne upon a car, and this usage was introduced into Europe, and continued down to the sixteenth century. The standard of the Saracens was thus borne. It was red, was drawn by eight horses, and so confident of victory were the soldiers so long as they saw it erect, that none would ever leave the field. It is asserted that when the sacred standard of Mohammed was captured by John Sobeiski, the Polish king, that so terrified were the Moslems at this unpropitious event, that they threw down their arms and fled in the utmost confusion. Sobeiski was victorious, and left two hundred thousand Turks dead upon the field. The ensign of the Venitians, in the time of the Doges, was borne upon a cart, drawn by oxen; and the main standard of Henry V. at the battle of Agincourt, was thus carried, the car being drawn by horses instead of oxen.

Standards of the Hebrew tribes.

The first record of the use of standards, in the Scriptures, is in the second chapter of Numbers, and second verse: "Every man of the children of Israel, shall pitch by his own standard, with the ensign of their father's house," &c. The above engraving is a copy of a picture by DE LOU- THERBOURG, representing the standards of the twelve tribes of Israel. The artist, unfurnished with data respecting the bearings of the standards of each of the tribes, has ingeniously composed the group, and their several bearings, in accordance with the blessing of Jacob pronounced upon his twelve sons. (See Genesis, chapter xlix.) To those who are unacquainted with the Hebrew, we give the following translation of the names, and by turning to the chapter alluded to, they will see how nearly the artist has portrayed the text.

The Tribes.	Standards.
Reuben,	Running Water.
Simeon,	Sword.
Manasseh,	Palm.
Judah,	Lion.
Zebulon,	Ship.
Issachar,	Ass.
Dan,	Serpent,
Gad,	Flag.
Asher,	Censer and Frankincense.
Napthali,	Hind.
Ephraim,	Grapes.
Benjamin,	Wolf.

The Jewish Rabbins, who profess to be very particular in their descriptions of everything relating to their ancient customs, have given minute details of the standards of the tribes, but unfortunately they themselves differ materially. They agree, however, that these ensigns were flags, having figures upon them emblematical of the pursuits or character of the several tribes. Some commentators suppose they were distinguished by difference in colors; others, that each bore a sign of the zodiac; and others again believe that they were simply flags, with the name of a tribe on each. DE LOUTHERBOURG has followed the text of Jacob's blessing, and has probably given us as correct a representation as can be obtained at this remote day.

Modern Oriental Standards.

OBSERVATIONS ON THE USE OF THE SLING, AS A WARLIKE WEAPON, AMONG THE ANCIENTS

WALTER HAWKINS

XII.—*Observations on the Use of the Sling, as a Warlike Weapon, among the Ancients: in a Letter from* WALTER HAWKINS, *Esq. F.S.A., addressed to Sir* HENRY ELLIS, *Secretary: accompanying a Present to the Society of a Leaden-pellet or Sling-bullet, found lodged in the Cyclopian Walls of Samé in Cephalonia.*

Read 26th November, 1846.

36, Finsbury Circus, 23rd November, 1846.

MY DEAR SIR HENRY,

As I believe that the collection of the Society of Antiquaries of London does not include a specimen of the Leaden-pellet or Sling-bullet of the Greeks, I do myself the honour to forward you one; of which, together with the accompanying drawing, I beg the Society's acceptance.

This specimen was found lodged in the Cyclopian walls of Samé in Cephalonia.

The determination of its date must depend upon the degree of probability which may be attached to the supposition that it was deposited there by one of the Achæan slingers from Ægium, Patræ, and Dyme, of whom there were one hundred in the army with which the Roman consul, M. Fulvius, reduced that place, after a siege of four months, B. C. 189. (Livy, xxxviii. 29.)

It will be observed that in shape it very nearly resembles an almond. It appears to exhibit on one side the characters ΦΑΙΝΩ or ΦΑΙΝΕ, commencing at the smaller or taper end, and extending to the larger, where they are slightly defaced in consequence of the forcible compression of the pellet from impact.

If the word be ΦΑΙΝΟΥ, or in the Ionic dialect ΦΑΙΝΕΩ, it will mean " Appear " or " Show yourself." The other side seems to have been without character or device. The superficial appearance which it now presents is the natural result of a long exposure to the atmosphere, which has produced an incrustation of carbonate of lead or white lead.

In collecting materials for the accompanying paper on the use of this species of missile among the ancients, I have availed myself of the assistance of friends whose attention has been especially directed to Greek history.

The importance of missiles in the military operations of the ancients is not to be estimated by that to which they have attained in modern warfare. The issue of a battle in ordinary cases depended on the conflict between the ὁπλῖται or heavy-armed soldiers; yet the ψιλοὶ or light troops, whose office it was to discharge stones, arrows, and darts, frequently rendered important service, whether as skirmishers, in driving the enemy from his battlements, in discomforting the wavering phalanx, or in dealing death against the fugitives. In this last capacity they constituted in some measure a substitute for cavalry, a description of troops in which the ancients were very deficient. But they afforded most effectual aid in rugged and mountainous places, where the regular troops, being unable to act, were destroyed, without the means of retaliating, by the slingers and archers on the surrounding heights. One cause of the undue depreciation of missile warfare amongst the Greeks, and of the disasters which its neglect entailed upon some of the finest armies, may be recognised in the pride of wealth or of valour which taught the citizen-soldier to regard the rank of the heavy-armed as the more honourable, whether on account of his more costly equipment, or of his more perilous post. The low estimation in which slingers were held is evinced by the fact that generals who wished to degrade or deteriorate a conquered people not unfrequently armed them with slings, and forbad them the use of any other weapon. This policy was adopted by Cyrus the Great (about B. C. 540) towards the Phrygians and Lydians. And Xenophon remarks that Cyrus considered the sling to be of all weapons the most dishonourable and servile; "For," he proceeds, "although slingers when combined with other forces are sometimes of the greatest service, yet not even a large body, if unsupported, could withstand the attack of a few men armed for close combat." The truth of this observation was evinced at the battle of Pharsalia, B. C. 48. Pompey's bow-men and slingers, of which description of troops there was a large number in his army, having been left exposed by the flight of the cavalry, were quickly cut to pieces by Cæsar's reserve. Again, Quintus

Curtius represents Alexander, before the battle of Gaugamela or Arbela, B. C. 331, as endeavouring to inspire his soldiers with contempt of their adversaries by reminding them that while some of them are armed with a javelin, others with a sling and stones, few are furnished with a full accoutrement. But, though such was the relative rank of slingers with respect to their comrades in arms, there were periods in which their importance in warfare was irresistibly forced upon the attention of the Greek generals and statesmen.

Our chief difficulty in tracing historically the use of the sling arises from the circumstance that under the name of "light troops" were comprehended several distinct classes of soldiers; the slingers, the bow-men, the javelin-men, and the stone-casters: and that the Greek historians more frequently use the general term than the specific denomination. We shall however, without professing to supply a complete history of the sling, be able to discover its chief epochs, and to collect accounts of some of the most important campaigns in which it was employed, together with some notices by ancient historians of its peculiar excellencies and deficiencies, as an engine of warfare.

The invention of the sling is attributed by Pliny to the Phœnicians, by Vegetius to the Baleares, (who were Phœnician colonists,) and by Strabo to the Ætolians. It was called in Greek σφενδόνη, and in Latin *funda*. It consisted of a thong of leather, a string of sinew, or a cord of twisted wool, hair, or hemp, of greatest width in the middle, where the stone or bullet rested; sometimes, however, a kind of cup was attached for the reception of the missile: of the two ends, the one which was to be held firmly in the hand usually terminated in a loop or handle. Slings varied in length according to circumstances, the shorter ones being used in the assault upon besieged towns, and the longer to gall an enemy from a distant eminence; for the projection of large stones they were constructed with two, three, or more cords. Cheapness and compactness were advantages offered by the sling over all other offensive weapons, and it often could be employed when other arms were unavailable (positis hastis). Virg. Æn. ix. 589. Stones or bullets could be projected from a sling to greater distance than either arrows from a bow, or javelins with the aid of a thong. The projectiles used in slings were in earlier times smooth pebbles, but afterwards leaden bullets; they were carried either in a bag (πήρα, *marsupium*) hung over the shoulder, or in the folds of the outer dress.

Most of these particulars are admirably illustrated by the representations of slingers upon the Egyptian monuments (as engraved in Wilkinson's Egypt, vol. i. 316), and by those upon the columns of Trajan and Antonine. (See Montfaucon and Bartoli.)

Many of the nations of antiquity are said to have attained most wonderful skill in the use of this weapon. Thus, the Benjamites, mentioned in the Book of Judges, could "sling stones at an hair-breadth and not miss." But amongst the most celebrated were the inhabitants of the Balearic isles (now Majorca and Minorca), whose name is derived by Polybius from βάλλειν, "to cast." Of this people Diodorus Siculus says that "they can hurl far larger stones than any others, and with so great force that the missile might be supposed to be projected from a catapult; and yet so accurate is their aim that they rarely miss their mark. This extraordinary skill is acquired by constant practice in their boyhood; for a custom obtains among this people of fastening pieces of bread upon poles, and compelling their children to win their meal by striking it from a distance with a sling-stone." They usually carried with them three σφενδόναι of different lengths, to serve either as bands or as slings; one of these was bound round the head, the second round the loins, and the third was carried in the hand. Livy informs us that at the time of the second Punic war (which was terminated B. C. 201) the Baleares bore no other arms but the sling; while in his own time, though it was still their chief weapon, it was not used exclusively. We learn from classical sources that the sling was in use amongst the Egyptians, Indians, Persians, Carduchi, Ilerdes and Spaniards, Cirtæi and Numidians, Belgæ, Gauls, Greeks, and Romans. Of all the Greeks the most noted slingers were the Achæans, Acarnanians, Ætolians, and Rhodians. The fame of the Achæans was perpetuated in the proverbial expression Αχαϊκον βέλος, "an Achæan hit." Livy relates that the Achæan boys were wont to practise slinging with smooth pebbles on the sea shore; "their sling," he says, "was made, not like the Balearic, of a single thong, but of three strengthened with stitching, and thus they effectually provided against the slipping of the bullet; they ply their slings with a longer range, and with surer aim, and greater force than the Baleares; they can hurl their missiles through small rings placed at a considerable distance, and hit not only the heads of the enemy, but any part of the face at which they choose to aim."

On the other hand Thucydides, four hundred years earlier, says, the Acarnanians had the reputation of being the most expert of all nations in this species of warfare. According to an ancient legend mentioned by Strabo, the Ætolians won their land from the original inhabitants through the issue in their favour of a single combat. Their own champion was armed with a sling (the use of which had been recently discovered among them), his adversary with a bow, and the longer range of the former weapon secured the victory to the Ætolian. The Athenians were at most periods very deficient in this branch of military art, and suffered in consequence several severe checks and defeats. The chief application of the sling among the Greeks was of course as a military engine; it was however also used for the sake of exercise; and Plato in his Laws advocates its adoption not by men only but by women, as a means of invigorating the body. The sling was assigned as an attribute to Nemesis, by which was signified that Divine justice reaches the guilty even from afar.

The earliest historical notice of the sling is about the date B. C. 1406; it is found in the Book of Judges, ch. xx. 16, where it is related that in the army of the Benjamites were " seven hundred chosen men, left-handed, every one of whom could sling stones at an hair-breadth."

The next allusion is in the well-known account of the death of the Philistine champion Goliath by the sling-stone of David. Again, it is said of some of the warriors who "came to David to Ziklag," B. C. 1058, "they were armed with bows, and could use both the right hand and the left in hurling stones, and shooting arrows out of a bow, even of Saul's brethren of Benjamin." Amongst the weapons which King Uzziah provided for his army, B. C. 810, were "bows and slings to cast stones" (or, as it is rendered in the margin, "stones of slings.") See also II Kings, ch. iii. 25.

From these passages it appears that the slingers occupied a far more honourable position in the Israelite armies than in those of the Greeks and Romans; we also have an intimation of a practice prevalent among this people of accustoming themselves to the use of either hand in slinging, and there is perhaps no need of attaching any other meaning than this to the expression "left-handed," in the first passage. The value which the Israelites assigned to the sling as an engine of destruction, may also be estimated from the frequent use in the prophecies of the expression to "sling-out" a people, as a synonym for total extermination.

Of the two Homeric passages which bear upon our present subject, (Il. xiii. 599, and xiii. 716,) the word σφενδόνη (a sling) occurs only in the first. It is there used in conjunction with the expression εὐστρόφῳ οἰὸς ἀώτῳ (a cord of twisted wool), which is again employed in line 716, without any explanatory adjunct. In the former passage Agenor is represented as bandaging the wounded arm of Helenus with a woollen σφενδόνη; and the Scholiast on this passage observes that the ancient slings were made of woollen cords. From the second passage we learn that Locrian slingers followed in the train of Ajax Oileus, and rendered service at the time of the attack on the ships by Hector and the Trojans. Their post in battle was in the rear of the army, whence they projected their missiles in security, and sorely galled the enemy's phalanx. The supposed date of these events is about B. C. 1184, three hundred years anterior to that of the poem in which they are related. In later times, the light troops were not unfrequently attached as servants to the *hoplites;* they commenced the battle by hurling their missiles on the advancing foe, and then retreated through the ranks to the rear of their own army. Thus, in the first engagement of the Athenians before Syracuse, B. C. 415, the stone-casters, slingers, and bow-men on either side, made the first assault, and then the trumpeters sounded the charge, and the *hoplites* advanced to the combat. Sometimes, however, at particular junctures, the light troops were again brought forward to assail the enemy with greater effect from a nearer position.

The conference between the Greek ambassadors and Gelo of Syracuse, relative to their contemplated alliance against Persia, B. C. 480, affords a good opportunity of estimating the usual numerical proportion of slingers to the rest of the army. The Syracusan auxiliary was intended to be as complete in all its appointments as the wealth of that potent tyrant could render it. The proposed complements of the several departments are thus given by Herodotus; 20,000 *hoplites*, 2,000 horse, 2,000 bow-men, 2,000 slingers, and 2,000 light horsemen.

The policy of Cyrus, which we have described above, rendered the proportion of slingers in his armies much larger; thus, on his advance upon Babylon, he was accompanied, says Xenophon, by a great multitude of horse and bow-men, and javelin-men, and by slingers innumerable. Again, in the disastrous expedition of the Athenians against Sicily, B. C. 415, the proportion of bow-men and slingers was made much larger than usual, in accordance with the requirements of Nicias, who demanded that a large body of these troops should be provided to form a counterpoise against the enemy's superiority in cavalry. The armament, therefore, was composed of 5,100 *hoplites*, 480 bow-men, 700 Rhodian slingers, 120 Megarian light troops, and 30 horse.

Two years afterwards Demosthenes, when on his way to join Nicias with the second armament, stopped to reinforce his troops with slingers and javelin-men from the territory of Acarnania. Reverting to a somewhat earlier period, we read that in the year B. C. 429 the Lacedemonians, having invaded Acarnania under the command of Cnemus, were completely foiled and compelled to retreat before the noted slingers of that country. The value of light troops in mountainous localities is well illustrated by the account of the reduction of Sphacteria, B. C. 425, when the redoubtable Spartans were cut off in detail by the arrows, javelins, stones, and slings of the enemy, without the opportunity of retaliating, or of reducing the contest to a pitched battle. Thucydides in detailing the circumstances of the calamitous expedition of Hippocrates into Bœotia, B. C. 424, relates that the Athenians were not at this period in the habit of including in their army any organised body of light troops, and in consequence were now totally unprovided with this description of soldiery; while on the other hand the Bœotian force was composed of 7,000 *hoplites*, 1,000 horse, 500 peltasts, and 10,000 light troops, which were stationed with the cavalry on the wings. Yet, after the defeat of the Athenians, and their retreat into Delium, the Bœotians sent for a reinforcement of javelin-men and slingers from the Malian Gulf, in the hope of speedily reducing the fortress by their aid, so great appears to have been the importance attached to missile warfare by this people.

Passing over other instances which might be alleged, we arrive now at the expedition of the Greeks in support of the pretensions of Cyrus the younger to the Persian throne. The general and historian of the famous retreat of the Ten Thousand, B. C. 401, relates that the Greeks suffered severely from the slingers in the army of Mithridates, while they themselves had no cavalry or slingers, and were unable to reach the enemy with their arrows and javelins. But Xenophon, having ascertained that there were in his army some Rhodians who understood the use of leaden sling-bullets, immediately organised a body of 200 men armed with these weapons. The employment of these Rhodians was attended with signal success; and they were able, says Xenophon, to project their missiles twice as far as the Persian slingers, who used large stones. Darius Codomannus in making his dispositions previous to the battle of Issus, B. C. 423, posted a force of 20,000 slingers and bow-men, with his cavalry, on the right wing, while in front of the whole army he placed 8,000 javelin-men and slingers. Hence it would seem that the policy of Cyrus was still pursued by the Persian Court.

At the same period we find mention of Acarnanian slingers in the army of Alexander. About B. C. 219, we read that Philip III. of Macedonia was supported by an auxiliary of 300 Achæan slingers; and we have already seen that the Romans had need of 100 slingers of the same nation to aid them in the reduction of Samé in Cephallenia, B. C. 189. It appears, therefore, that the Acarnanians and Achæans retained down to a late period their ancient celebrity as slingers.

The early notices of the sling which we have instanced have been chosen, not so much for their historial sequence, as for their importance in illustrating the mode in which this weapon was generally employed.

Towards the close of the fifth century before Christ, the use of sling-stones began to be superseded by that of leaden bullets, and from this period downwards the latter missiles are frequently mentioned both by Greek and Roman historians. But before we proceed to describe these bullets more minutely, we will adduce a few examples of the use of the sling from Roman history. Livy informs us that Hannibal, previously to his descent upon Italy, B. C. 219, provided for the safety of Africa by sending over 870 Balearic slingers; another body of light-armed Baleares accompanied his own army, and 500 were left with Hasdrubal in Spain. Again, in B. C. 206, when Mago attempted to land upon the greater of the Balearic islands (Majorca), the inhabitants hurled their sling-stones in such numbers upon his ships that he was not able even to enter the harbour. Cæsar employed Balearic slingers with eminent success in the Gallic war, and on one occasion he routed the foe by the employment of sling-stones of a pound weight, and of bullets. When he invaded Britain, B. C. 55, he disposed his slingers and other light troops on the decks of his ships-of-war for the purpose of terrifying the Britons, and covering the landing of his troops.

In the year A. D. 16, Germanicus, by a skilful disposition of his slingers, obtained a victory over the Germans in a rugged and woody country, where a hand-to-hand engagement would probably have entailed a defeat. Again, when Corbulo was attacking one of the fortresses of Armenia, A. D. 59, he posted his slingers so as to gall the enemy at different points, and thus prevented their rendering succour to one another.

Slings were also used with remarkable success against elephants, which, terrified as much by the whizzing sound as by the actual blow, often turned upon their masters and committed great havoc. We might easily enlarge the number of our quotations, but enough have been already adduced to illustrate this portion of our subject.

We have before remarked, that towards the close of the fifth century plummets or leaden bullets began to supersede the ancient sling-stones. The name given to these missiles by the Greeks was μολυβδίδες, μολύβδαιναι, or σφαῖραι μολύβδιναι, "leaden balls," and by the Romans *glandes*, "acorns." This latter name was derived from their shape, which very nearly resembles that of the acorn, the olive, or the almond, and was calculated to experience a comparatively slight resistance from the atmosphere. Stores of these pellets or sling-bullets were kept in the arsenals for future use: sometimes, however, the metal was fused and bullets cast in the camp when an engagement was already impending, as was the case in Cæsar's African war, B. C. 46. The bullets were generally ornamented with some device, such as a thunderbolt, a star, or an arrow-head, or with characters, as the word ΦΑΙΝΕ, "Appear;" ΔΕΞΑΙ, "Take this;" ΒΑCΙΛΕΩ(C), "The King's;" ΛΗΓΕ, "Desist." Sometimes, also, we find on bullets the names of the generals, as for instance, ΚΛΕΟΝΙΚΟΥ, "Cleonicus'," ΚΑΛΙΣΤΡΑΤΟΥ, "Calistratus'"; and again, the names of Philip and Perdiccas, or those again of the contending nations, or merely a monogram or single letter, of which, after the lapse of so many years, we cannot now hope to obtain a solution. The characters appear generally to have been in relief, and to have read from the smaller end to the larger, where they are often defaced in consequence of the collision of the bullet with some hard object.

Sling-bullets sometimes weighed as much as an Attic pound, though the usual weights of the extant specimens are between $1\frac{1}{2}$ and $3\frac{1}{2}$ ounces. Specimens have been found on the plains of Marathon, in Cephallenia, Ithaca, and Corcyra, at Athens, and in the channel of the Ilissus. There was another use to which these leaden projectiles were applied (at any rate in later times), which we have not yet mentioned; namely, the communication of warning or of intelligence, as for instance by secret friends in the enemy's camp. Thus, when Sylla laid siege to Athens, and the city was at length reduced to the last stage of famine, a secret friend within the walls informed the Roman general that on the following night Archelaus (the General of Mithridates) intended to introduce some provisions from the Piræus. This information was inscribed on a sling-bullet, which Appian calls πεσσός, (an oval body, whether of stone or lead); and Sylla was thus enabled to intercept both the supplies and those who had charge of them. They were similarly employed on several distinct occasions during Cæsar's war against Cnæius Pompeius in Spain. At a subsequent period these missiles, as well as the soldiers who projected them, seem to have acquired the nic-name of "Martiobarbuli," a word which has been derived from *barbus*, "a barbel," and said to mean the dainty fare or tit-bits of Mars.

A favourite notion of the Roman poets, and one that must be recorded not as a mere poetical extravagance, but rather as a somewhat hyperbolical expression of a matured opinion, was that the bullet was heated and almost liquified by its friction with the air. Thus Virgil, in the 9th Æneid, line 589,

> "Stridentem fundam positis Mezentius armis,
> Ipse ter adductâ circum caput egit habenâ;
> Et media adversi liquefacto tempora plumbo
> Diffidit."

Which Dryden translates:

> "Him when he spy'd from far, the Tuscan King
> Laid by the lance, and took him to the sling,
> Thrice whirl'd the thong around his head, and threw
> The heated lead, half-melted as it flew," &c.

Again, Lucretius instances the "melting" of the sling-bullet in support of the assertion that all things are heated by motion.—Book vi. 177.

> "Ut omnia motu
> Percalefacta vides ardescere : plumbea vero
> Glans etiam longo cursu volvunda liquescit."

And Ovid. Metam. ii. 727,

> "Non secus exarsit, quam cum Balearica plumbum
> Funda jacet, volat illud, et incandescit eundo,
> Et quos non habuit, sub nubibus invenit ignes."

And lastly Lucan, Phars. vii. 513,

> "Saxa volant spatioque solutæ
> Aeris, et calido liquefactæ pondere glandes."

Specimens of sling-bullets with Roman characters are far more scarce than those with the Greek letters. The largest number have been found at Florence, where (as is conjectured) there was formerly a Roman arsenal. Amongst the devices in Roman characters may be mentioned the following: *Feri*, "Strike;" *Fugitivi peritis*, "Ye perish in your flight;" *Ital. et Gall.* "The Italians and the Gauls." And among the ruins of Eryx, to the eastward of Trapani, (the ancient Drepanum,) many leaden bullets for slings are found, some of which are inscribed with imprecations. (See Captain Smyth's "Sicily and its Islands," page 242.) We may instance one of these inscriptions, which is translated: "Your heart for Cerberus." Many of the ancient sling-bullets which are still preserved are incrusted with carbonate of lead, from the natural effects of long exposure to the atmosphere, as appears by the specimen presented, and sometimes with yellow oxide of lead or litharge, where they have been submitted to the more direct action of the sun's rays.

With the mention of a few peculiar applications of the sling, we will conclude our historical sketch of the use of this weapon amongst the ancients. Pellets of a kind of porcelain or earthenware, and moulded like sling-bullets, were sometimes used; they were discharged when red hot. Quintus Cicero, Cæsar's Lieutenant in

Gaul, employed these formidable missiles against the Nervii, B. C. 57. A new species of sling was employed by Perseus, King of Macedonia, against the Romans, B. C. 171. It is called *cestrosphendone* by Polybius and Livy, and was constructed to project a kind of dart *(cestrum)* of the length of half an ell. It contributed much to the discomfiture of the Romans at Sycurium in Thessaly. Vegetius describes a species of sling in use in his time (A. D. 3), which is more familiar to us as a weapon of the middle ages; it is the *fustibulus* or "staff-sling," and is described by that author as consisting of a staff of four feet in length, to which was attached a sling of leather. It was wielded with both hands. But stones were hurled not only from slings, but also with the naked hand. The armies of the ancients, especially those of the Greeks, frequently included large numbers of stone-throwers, λιθοβόλοι or πετροβόλοι. And in Homer we constantly read of great execution being done by the χερμάδια or large stones thus projected. Again, as the advancement of the arts introduced new weapons, engines were employed for the projection of stones and darts. The slingers (σφενδονῆται, *funditores)* must be distinguished from the stone-throwers on the one hand, and on the other from the engine-men, (ἀφεται, *balistarii,*) who by aid of the balista (in Greek πετροβόλος) threw stones of half a hundred weight, a whole hundred weight, and even three hundred weight.

We now pass to mediæval and modern times.

The sling has often been assigned to the ancient Britons; but there appears to be no adequate foundation for this supposition. The Saxons, however, were celebrated for their skill in the use of this weapon; and the Anglo-Norman army seems always to have included an organised body of slingers; but the use of the sling gradually became obsolete, though it was retained for a long time as a means of amusement and exercise. We have however evidence of its employment in war as late as the end of the fourteenth century, in the ballad entitled "A Tale of King Edward and the Shepherd;" and at the commencement of the fifteenth century, in the following passage from a poem, called "Knyghthode and Batayle," quoted by Strutt in his "Sports and Pastimes."

> " Use eek the cast of stone, with sling or honde
> It falleth ofte, yf other shot there none is,
> Men harneysed in steel may not withstonde
> The multitude and mighty cast of stonys;
> And stonys in effect are every where,
> And slynges are not noyous for to bear.'

The box in which, for the sake of protection, the pellet now submitted to the Society has been inclosed, is constructed of the wood of the redoubtable Téméraire. Some few particulars respecting this vessel have been engraved, and a copy has been placed in the lid of the box.

I have the honour to subscribe myself,

My dear Sir Henry,

With much respect, yours very sincerely,

WALTER HAWKINS.

Coachwhip Publications
CoachwhipBooks.com

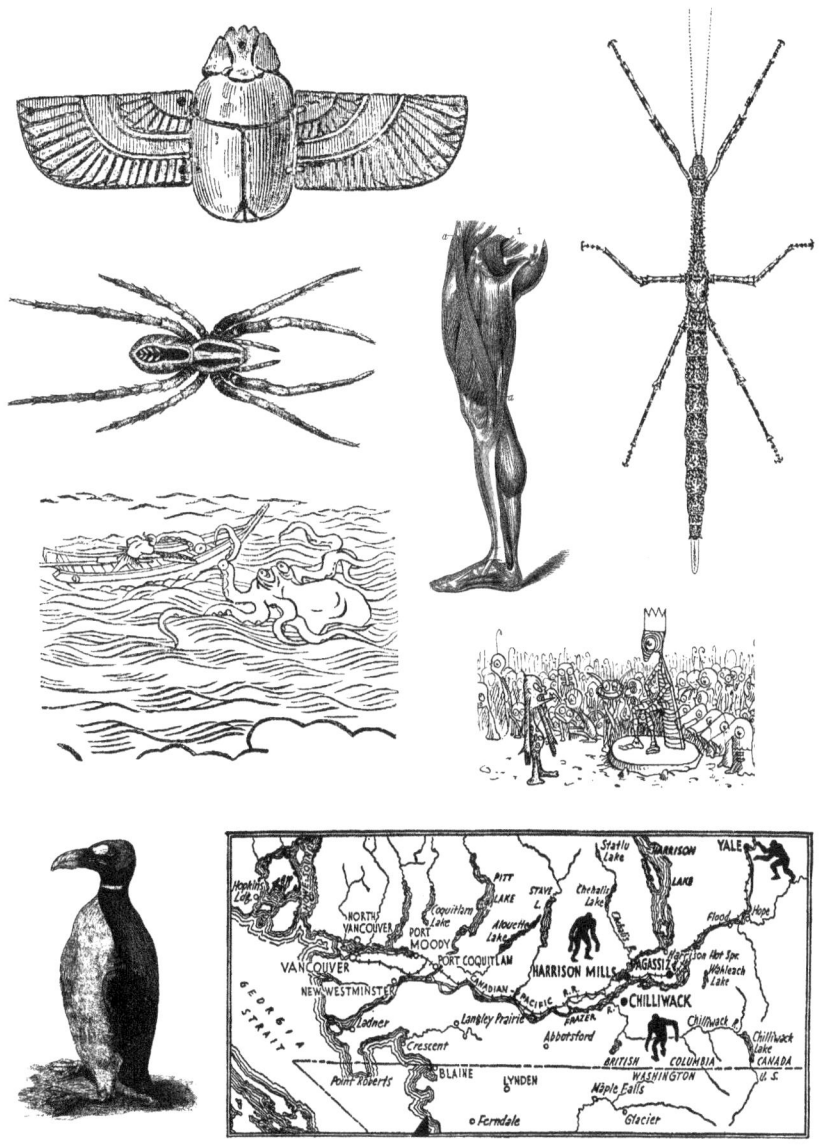

Coachwhip Publications
Also Available

Coachwhip Publications
CoachwhipBooks.com

www.ingramcontent.com/pod-product-compliance
Lightning Source LLC
Chambersburg PA
CBHW081354040426
42450CB00016B/3442